PASS THE NEW CITIZENSHIP TEST
THIRD EDITION

Angelo Tropea

ISBN-13: 978-1499259322   ISBN-10: 1499259328

Published by Angelo Tropea

For all immigrants...all over the world.

Reader comments on prior edition:

*"My wife teaches a citizenship course and both she and her students love this book!
Good for review by natural citizens, too!"*

"I needed this book to study for my citizenship test. I passed with flying colors. I recommend it to anyone."

"We use this book for our foreign nationals that are becoming US Citizens. They all find it very helpful."

*"One cannot go wrong with this book if you want to pass your citizenship test.
The 100 questions comes in various forms. It covers all the history, government and geography questions as well as preparation for the English writing and reading....if one is not fluent in English."*

"This has a good explanation of each question and the book has 3 ways to explain and allow practice of each question. Seems to be better than other choices on Amazon."

CONTENTS

———————

THE CIVICS, READING AND WRITING TESTS

1. Civics (History, Government and Geography) Questions

You will be asked up to 10 questions from the 100 questions that the government has published. All the questions and answers are included in this book. To pass this part of the test, you must answer correctly at least 6 of the questions.

Note: Applicants who are 65 or older when they file the Application for Naturalization, Form N-400, and who have been legal permanent residents of the United States for 20 or more years, may qualify for special consideration on the civics test. They only need to study 20 questions and answers that are marked with a (***) in this book. (Question #: 6, 11, 13, 17, 20, 27, 28, 44, 45, 49, 54, 56, 70, 75, 78, 85, 94, 95, 97, 99)

2. English writing section

You will be asked to write three (3) sentences containing specific words that the government has announced. All the words (less than 100 words) are listed in this book on page 21. To pass this writing section, you must write one sentence out of the three sentences in a manner that is understandable to the USCIS Officer.

3. English reading section

You will be asked to read three (3) sentences containing specific words (less than 100) that the government has announced. All the words are listed in this book on page 22. To pass this reading section, you must read one sentence out of the three sentences in a manner suggesting to the USCIS Officer that you appear to understand the meaning of the sentence.

For complete information on filing to become a Naturalized U.S. Citizen and test requirements and scoring guidelines, please visit: www.uscis.gov/portal/site/uscis

HOW TO USE THIS BOOK

1. Civics (History, Government and Geography) Questions

Each page has 6 study cards. Each of the first 2 cards (top of page) have one of the 100 civics questions you may be asked. Read the question out loud and then try to answer it out loud. This way you will get used to the sound of the question and the sound of the answer. This will help you remember the question and answer. If you don't know the answer, turn the page and look at the answer. Study the questions every day. By doing this you will find that even the difficult questions become easy after a while. Have a friend or relative who speaks English study with you. Let your friend or relative read the question, and then try to answer it. Ask your friend or relative if you are pronouncing the answer correctly. Say the answer over and over until you are comfortable with it and have it completely memorized.

2. English writing section

The middle 2 study card on each page help you practice writing English. Read the words, or better yet have a friend or relative read them. On a separate piece of paper, write the words, either in printed letters or in long hand (script). Before turning the page, try to make a sentence using all of the words. Write the sentence. Check to see if you spelled each word correctly. Does your sentence match the sentence on the next page (more than one sentence is possible). Have a friend or relative read the sentence out loud and then practice writing it. As in everything else, the more you practice, the better you will do.

3. English reading section

On the bottom 2 cards on each page (closest to the bottom of the page) there are several words. Read the words. When you think you can read each word, turn the page and read the sentence in the study card near the bottom of the page. If possible, study with a friend or relative. Have them comment on the way you are pronouncing the words. Listen carefully when your friend or relative says the words.

CIVICS (HISTORY & GOVERNMENT) QUESTIONS

1. What is the supreme law of the land?
    the Constitution

2. What does the Constitution do?
    sets up the government,
    defines the government,
    protects basic rights of Americans

3. The idea of self-government is in the first three words of the Constitution. What are these words?
    We the People

4. What is an amendment?
    a change (to the Constitution),
    an addition (to the Constitution)

5. What do we call the first ten amendments to the Constitution?
    the Bill of Rights

6. What is one right or freedom from the First Amendment? (***)
    Speech, religion, assembly, press, petition the government

7. How many amendments does the Constitution have?
    twenty-seven (27)

8. What did the Declaration of Independence do?
    announced our independence (from Great Britain)
    declared our independence (from Great Britain)
    said that the United States is free (from Great Britain)

9. What are two rights in the Declaration of Independence?
    Life, liberty, pursuit of happiness

10. What is freedom of religion?
You can practice any religion, or not practice a religion.

11. What is the economic system in the United States? (***)
capitalist economy, market economy

12. What is the "rule of law"?
Everyone must follow the law.
Leaders must obey the law.
Government must obey the law.
No one is above the law.

13. Name one branch or part of the government. (***)
Congress (legislative), President (executive), the courts (judicial)

14. What stops one branch of government from becoming too powerful?
checks and balances, separation of powers

15. Who is in charge of the executive branch?
the President

16. Who makes federal laws?
Congress,
Senate and House (of Representatives),
(U.S. or national) Legislature

17. What are the two parts of the U.S. Congress? (***)
Senate and House (of Representatives)

18. How many U.S. Senators are there?
one hundred (100)

19. We elect a U.S. Senator for how many years?
six (6)

20. Who is one of your state's U.S. Senators now? (***)
Answers depends upon which state you live in. (District of Columbia residents and residents of U.S. territories should answer that D.C. (or the territory where the applicant lives) has no U.S. Senators.)

21. The House of Representatives has how many voting members?
four hundred thirty-five (435)

22. We elect a U.S. Representative for how many years?
two (2)

23. Name your U.S. Representative.
Answers depend on where you live. (Residents of territories with Non-voting delegates or resident commissioners may provide the name of that Delegate or Commissioner. Also acceptable is any statement that the territory has no (voting) Representatives in Congress.)

24. Who does a U.S. Senator represent?
all people of the state

25. Why do some states have more Representatives than other states?
(because of) the state's population,
(because) they have more people
(because) some states have more people

26. We elect a President for how many years?
four (4)

27. In what month do we vote for President? (***)
November

28. What is the name of the President of the United States now? (***)
Barack Obama, Obama

29. What is the name of the Vice President of the United States now?
Joseph R. Biden, Jr., Joe Biden, Biden

30. If the President can no longer serve, who becomes President?
   the Vice President

31. If both the President and the Vice President can no longer serve, who becomes President?
   the Speaker of the House

32. Who is the Commander in Chief of the military?
   the President

33. Who signs bills to become laws?
   the President

34. Who vetoes bills?
   the President

35. What does the President's Cabinet do?
   advises the President

36. What are two Cabinet-level positions?
   Secretary of Agriculture, Secretary of Commerce, Secretary of Defense, Secretary of Education, Secretary of Energy, Secretary of Health and Human Services, Secretary of Homeland Security, Secretary of Housing and Urban Development, Secretary of the Interior, Secretary of Labor, Secretary of State, Secretary of Transportation, Secretary of the Treasury, Secretary of Veterans Affairs, Attorney General, Vice President

37. What does the judicial branch do?
   reviews laws, explains laws, resolves disputes (disagreements), decides if a law goes against the Constitution

38. What is the highest court in the United States?
   the Supreme Court

39. How many justices are on the Supreme Court?
   nine (9)

40. Who is the Chief Justice of the United States now?
John Roberts (John G. Roberts, Jr.)

41. Under our Constitution, some powers belong to the federal government. What is one power of the federal government?
to print money, to declare war, to create an army, to make treaties

42. Under our Constitution, some powers belong to the states. What is one power of the states?
provide schooling and education, provide protection (police, provide safety (fire departments), give a driver's license, approve zoning and land use

43. Who is the Governor of your state now?
Answers will vary. (District of Columbia residents should answer that D.C. does not have a Governor.)

44. What is the capital of your state? (***)
Answers vary. (District of Columbia residents should answer that D.C. is not a state and does not have a capital. Residents of U.S. territories should name the capital of the territory.)

45. What are the two major political parties in the United States? (***)
Democratic and Republican

46. What is the political party of the President now?
Democratic (Party)

47. What is the name of the Speaker of the House of Representatives now?
(John) Boehner

48. There are four amendments to the Constitution about who can vote. Describe one of them.
Citizens eighteen (18) and older (can vote).
You don't have to pay (a poll tax) to vote.
Any citizen can vote. (Women and men can vote.)
A male citizen of any race (can vote).

49. What is one responsibility that is only for United States citizens? (***)
serve on a jury,
vote in a federal election

50. Name one right only for United States citizens.
vote in a federal election,
run for federal office

51. What are two rights of everyone living in the United States?
freedom of expression, freedom of speech, freedom of assembly, freedom to petition the government, freedom of worship, the right to bear arms

52. What do we show loyalty to when we say the Pledge of Allegiance?
the United States, the flag

53. What is one promise you make when you become a United States citizen?
give up loyalty to other countries, defend the Constitution and laws of the United States, obey the laws of the United States, serve in the U.S. military (if needed), serve (do important work for) the nation (if needed), be loyal to the United States

54. How old do citizens have to be to vote for President? (***)
eighteen (18) and older

55. What are two ways that Americans can participate in their democracy?
Vote, join a political party, help with a campaign, join a civic group, join a community group, give an elected official your opinion on an issue, call Senators and Representatives, publicly support or oppose an issue or policy, run for office, write to a newspaper

56. When is the last day you can send in federal income tax forms? (***)
April 15

57. When must all men register for the Selective Service?
at age eighteen (18), between eighteen (18) and twenty-six (26)

58. What is one reason colonists came to America?
Freedom, political liberty, religious freedom, economic opportunity, practice their religion, escape persecution

59. Who lived in America before the Europeans arrived?
American Indians, Native Americans

60. What group of people was taken to America and sold as slaves?
Africans, people from Africa

61. Why did the colonists fight the British?
because of high taxes (taxation without representation), because the British army stayed in their houses (boarding, quartering), because they didn't have self-government

62. Who wrote the Declaration of Independence?
(Thomas) Jefferson

63. When was the Declaration of Independence adopted?
July 4, 1776

64. There were 13 original states. Name three.
New Hampshire, Massachusetts, Rhode Island, Connecticut, New York, New Jersey, Pennsylvania, Delaware, Maryland, Virginia, North Carolina, South Carolina, Georgia

65. What happened at the Constitutional Convention?
The Constitution was written.
The Founding Fathers wrote the Constitution.

66. When was the Constitution written?
1787

67. The Federalist Papers supported the passage of the U.S. Constitution. Name one of the writers.
(James) Madison, (Alexander) Hamilton, (John) Jay, Publius

68. What is one thing Benjamin Franklin is famous for?
U.S. diplomat, oldest member of the Constitutional Convention, first Postmaster General of the United States, writer of "Poor Richard's Almanac", started the first free libraries

69. Who is the "Father of Our Country"?
(George) Washington

70. Who was the first President? (***)
(George) Washington

71. What territory did the United States buy from France in 1803?
the Louisiana Territory, Louisiana

72. Name one war fought by the United States in the 1800s.
War of 1812, Mexican-American War, Civil War, Spanish-American War

73. Name the U.S. war between the North and the South.
the Civil War, the War between the States

74. Name one problem that led to the Civil War.
Slavery, economic reasons, states' rights

75. What was one important thing that Abraham Lincoln did? (***)
freed the slaves (Emancipation Proclamation), saved (or preserved) the Union, led the United States during the Civil War

76. What did the Emancipation Proclamation do?
freed the slaves, freed slaves in the Confederacy, freed slaves in the Confederate states, freed slaves in most Southern states

77. What did Susan B. Anthony do?
fought for women's rights, fought for civil rights

78. Name one war fought by the United States in the 1900s. (***)
World War I, World War II, Korean War, Vietnam, War, (Persian) Gulf War

79. Who was President during World War I?
(Woodrow) Wilson

80. Who was President during the Great Depression and World War II?
(Franklin) Roosevelt

81. Who did the United States fight in World War II?
Japan, Germany, and Italy

82. Before he was President, Eisenhower was a general. What war was he in?
World War II

83. During the Cold War, what was the main concern of the United States?
Communism

84. What movement tried to end racial discrimination?
civil rights (movement)

85. What did Martin Luther King, Jr. do? (***)
fought for civil rights, worked for equality for all Americans

86. What major event happened on Sept. 11, 2001, in the United States?
Terrorists attacked the United States.

87. Name one American Indian tribe in the United States.
Cherokee, Navajo, Sioux, Chippewa, Choctaw, Pueblo, Apache, Iroquois, Creek, Blackfeet, Seminole, Cheyenne, Arawak, Shawnee, Mohegan, Huron, Oneida, Lakota, Crow, Teton, Hopi, Inuit

88. Name one of the two longest rivers in the United States.
Missouri (River), Mississippi (River)

89. What ocean is on the West Coast of the United States?
Pacific (Ocean)

90. What ocean is on the East Coast of the United States?
   Atlantic (Ocean)

91. Name one U.S. territory.
   Puerto Rico, U.S. Virgin Islands, American Samoa, Northern Mariana Islands, Guam

92. Name one state that borders Canada.
   Maine, New Hampshire, Vermont, New York, Pennsylvania, Ohio, Michigan, Minnesota, North Dakota, Montana, Idaho, Washington, Alaska

93. Name one state that borders Mexico.
   California, Arizona, New Mexico, Texas

94. What is the capital of the United States? (***)
   Washington, D.C.

95. Where is the Statue of Liberty? (***)
   New York (Harbor), Liberty Island, New Jersey, near New York City, and on the Hudson (River).

96. Why does the flag have 13 stripes?
   because there were 13 original colonies, because the stripes represent the original colonies

97. Why does the flag have 50 stars? (***)
   because there is one star for each state, because each star represents a state, because there are 50 states

98. What is the name of the national anthem?
   The Star-Spangled Banner

99. When do we celebrate Independence Day? (***)
   July 4

100. Name two national U.S. holidays.
New Year's Day, Martin Luther King, Jr. Day, Presidents' Day,
Memorial Day, Independence Day, Labor Day, Columbus Day,
Veterans Day, Thanksgiving, Christmas

---

100 QUESTIONS IN LOGICAL (HISTORICAL) ORDER

This section contains the same 100 preceding questions, but in a logical order which will help you to remember them. The **answers** to the questions are displayed in **bold letters** so that you will know what information is actually asked by the examiner.

Christopher Columbus discovered America (the New World) in 1492.

The people who lived in America before Europeans arrived were the American Indians, the native Americans. (Ques.59)
They lived in many places in different groups called tribes.
Some of the tribes were: Cherokee, Navajo, Sioux, Chippewa, Choctaw, Pueblo, Apache, Iroquois, Creek, Blackfeet, Seminole, Cheyenne, Arawak, Shawnee, Mohegan, Huron, Oneida, Lakota, Crow, Teton, Hopi, Inuit. (Ques.87)

In Europe in the 1500's and later years there were not many liberties or freedoms or economic opportunities for people to get ahead and live a comfortable life. Because of this, many people (which we call "settlers" or "colonists") came to the New World. Some settled in South America, the Caribbean Islands, and some settled in North America – what we now know as Canada and the United States.
Colonists came to America to: get freedom, political liberty, economic opportunity, practice their religion, escape persecution. (Ques.58)
Colonists from Great Britain and other European countries settled in the eastern part of what is now the United States. At first they formed small villages and towns. Slowly the population grew and spread further inland. Great Britain governed the area which we now refer to as the "thirteen colonies."

As a result of the war between the colonists and Great Britain, these thirteen colonies formed into the first 13 American states.

There were thirteen (13) original states: New Hampshire, Massachusetts, Rhode Island, Connecticut, New York, New Jersey, Pennsylvania, Delaware, Maryland, Virginia, North Carolina, South Carolina, Georgia. (Ques.64)

On July 4, 1776, people from 13 British colonies in North America signed a paper called the Declaration of Independence. This paper stated that the 13 colonies were no longer colonies of England and that they were free and independent.

The Declaration of Independence was written by Thomas Jefferson. (Ques.62) Years later, Thomas Jefferson became a President of the United States.
The Declaration of Independence was adopted on July 4, 1776. (Ques.63)
The Declaration of Independence: 1) announced our independence (from Great Britain), 2) declared our independence (from Great Britain), 3) said that the United States is free (from Great Britain). (Ques.8)

The colonists fought the British because of high taxes (taxation without representation), because the British army stayed in their houses (boarding, quartering), because they didn't have self-government. (Ques.61)
Two rights in the Declaration of Independence are life, liberty, and the pursuit of happiness. (Ques.9)

Great Britain did not agree with the colonists trying to be independent from Great Britain. The American Revolutionary war was a result of Britain trying to recapture the colonies.

The Father of Our Country is George Washington. (Ques.69) He led the revolutionary army against Great Britain. He also later became the first President of the United States. **The first President was George Washington.** (Ques.70)

In 1787 representatives from the 13 colonies wrote the constitution. Soon after that they added 10 changes to the constitution. These changes are called "amendments" to the constitution.
The Constitution was written in 1787. (Ques.66)
At the Constitutional Convention the constitution was written (the founding fathers wrote the constitution). (Ques.65)

The federalist papers supported the passage of the Constitution. **The writers of the Federalist Papers were: (James) Madison, (Alexander) Hamilton, (John) Jay, Publius.** (Ques.67)

Because there was disagreement as to what the Constitution should contain, some people proposed that the original Constitution should be changed, or enlarged. They proposed changes which we call "amendments" to the Constitution.

An amendment is a change to the Constitution. (Ques.4)
An amendment is an addition to the Constitution. (Ques.4)

We call the first ten amendments to the Constitution the "Bill of Rights."
(Ques.5). The constitution and the amendments say many things, including that all people have the equal rights and that the government is elected by the people.

The Constitution is the supreme law of the land. (Ques.1)
The Constitution sets up the government. (Ques.2)
The Constitution defines the government. (Ques.2)
The Constitution protects basic rights of Americans. (Ques.2)
One freedom guaranteed us by the Constitution is freedom of religion.

Freedom of religion means that you can practice any religion, or not practice a religion. (Ques.10)

The idea of self-government is in the first three words of the Constitution.
These three words are "We the People." (Ques.3)
The first amendment guarantees certain rights or freedoms.
One right or freedom from the First Amendment is: speech, religion, assembly, press, petition the government. (Ques.6)

In the United States we agree that we must live by the rule of law.
The "rule of law" means that: everyone must follow the law, leaders must follow the law, no one is above the law. (Ques.12)
As the years passed, more amendments were added to the Constitution. Today the Constitution has twenty-seven (27) amendments. (Ques.7)

Under the Constitution some powers belong to the federal government. These powers are to print money, to declare war, to create an army, to make treaties. (Ques.41)
Under the Constitution some powers belong to the states. These powers are provide schooling and education, provide protection (police), provide safety (fire departments), give a driver's license, approve zoning and land use. (Ques.42)

There are four amendments to the Constitution about who can vote: 1) citizens (18) and older can vote, 2) you don't have to pay a poll tax to vote, 3) any citizen, man or woman, can vote, 4) a male citizen of any race can vote. (Ques.48)

To make sure that no one person or agency has too much power, our government is divided into three (3) parts, or branches.
The branches of our government are: Congress, legislative (President, executive), the courts (judicial). (Ques.13)
The checks and balances, or separation of powers among the three branches stops one branch of government from becoming too powerful. (Ques.14)

The President is in charge of the executive branch of government. (Ques.15)

The President is elected for four (4) years. (Ques.26)
We elect the President in the month of November. (Ques.27)
The President is Commander in Chief of the military. (Ques.32)
The President signs bills to become laws. (Ques.33)
The President can veto bills and stop them from becoming law. (Ques.33)
The President appoints people to help him run the government. The top people become part of his cabinet.

The President's cabinet advises the President. (Ques.5)
The following are Cabinet-level positions: Secretary of Agriculture, Secretary of Commerce, Secretary of Defense, Secretary of Education, Secretary of Energy, Secretary of Health And Human Services, Secretary of Homeland Security, Secretary of Housing and Urban Development, Secretary of the Interior, Secretary of Labor,

Secretary of State, Secretary of Transportation, Secretary of The Treasury, Secretary of Veterans Affairs, Attorney General, Vice President. (Ques.36)

The name of the President of the United States now (Jan. 2014) is Barack Obama. (Ques.28)
The name of the Vice President now (Jan. 2014) is Joseph R. Biden, Jr., Joe Biden, Biden. (Ques.29)

If the President can no longer serve, the Vice President becomes President. (Ques.30)
If both the President and the Vice President can no longer serve, the Speaker of the House becomes President. (Ques.31)

The judicial branch: reviews laws, explains laws, resolves disputes (disagreements), decides if a law goes against the Constitution. (Ques.37)
The highest court in the United States is the Supreme Court. (Ques.38)
There are nine (9) justices on the Supreme Court. (Ques.39)
The Chief Justice of the United States is John G. Roberts, Jr. (Ques.40)

The two parts of the U.S. Congress are the Senate and the House (of Representatives). (Ques.17)
Federal laws are made by Congress (Senate and House of Representatives), also known as the U.S. or national legislature). (Ques.16)

There are one hundred (100) U.S. senators. (Ques.18)
U.S. Senators represent all the people of their state. (Ques.24)
U.S. Senators are elected for six (6) years. (Ques.19)

The House of Representatives has 435 voting members. (Ques.21)

U.S. Representatives are elected for two (2) years. (Ques.22)
Some states have more Representatives than other states because of the state's population, because they have more people, because some states have more people. (Ques.25)

In 1803 the United States bought from France the Louisiana Territory, Louisiana. (Ques.71). As the years passed, more states were added to the United States of America. Some disagreed about such things as slavery.

Africans (people from Africa) were taken to America and sold as slaves. (Ques.60)
Problems that led to the Civil War were: slavery, economic reasons, states' rights. (Ques.74)
The U.S. war between the North and the South is called the Civil War, the War between the States. (Ques.73)
The Civil War lasted from 1861 to 1865. During the civil war, the President was Abraham Lincoln.

The Emancipation Proclamation was issued by President Lincoln. It freed the slaves, freed slaves in Confederate states, freed slaves in the Confederacy, freed slaves in most Southern states. (Ques.76)
President Abraham Lincoln: freed the slaves (Emancipation Proclamation), saved (or preserved) the Union, led the United States during the Civil War. (Ques.75)

In the 1800's the United States fought several wars: the War of 1812, the Mexican-American War, the Civil War, the Spanish-American War. (Ques.72)

In the 1900's the United States fought several wars: World War I, World War II, Korean War, Vietnam War, (Persian) Gulf War. (Ques.78)
During the First World War, the President was (Woodrow) Wilson. (Ques.79)

During the Great Depression and World War II, the President was (Franklin) Roosevelt. (Ques.80)

During World War II, the United States fought Japan, Italy, and Germany. (Ques.81)
During World War II, Eisenhower was a general. (Ques.82)

During the Cold War, the main concern of the United States was Communism. (Ques.83)

The civil rights movement tried to end discrimination. (Ques.84)

During our history there were many leaders trying to improve our country. **Martin Luther King fought for civil rights, worked for equality of all Americans.** (Ques.85)

On September 11, 2001, terrorists attacked the United States. (Ques.86)

Benjamin Franklin is famous for being a U.S. diplomat, the oldest member of the Constitutional Convention, first Postmaster General of the United States, writer of "Poor Richard's Almanac, and for starting the first free libraries. (Ques.68)

Susan B. Anthony fought for women's rights, fought for civil rights. (Ques.77)

The two major political parties in the United States are the Republican party and the Democratic party. (Ques.45)
The political party of the President now (Barack Obama) is the Democratic party. (Ques.46)
The name of the Speaker of the House of Representatives now is (John) Boehner (Jan. 2014). (Ques.47)

A responsibility of an American citizen is 1) to vote in a federal election, 2) serve on a jury. (Ques.49)
A right of an American Citizen is 1) to vote in a federal election, 2) run for federal office. (Ques.50)
A citizen has to be eighteen (18) or older to vote for President. (Ques.54)
Two rights of everyone living in the United States are: freedom of expression, freedom of speech, freedom of assembly, freedom to petition the government, freedom of worship, the right to bear arms. (Ques.51)

One promise you make when you become a United States citizen is 1) give up loyalty to other countries, 2) defend the Constitution and laws of the United States, 3) obey the laws of the United States, 4) serve in the U.S. military (if needed), 5) serve (do important work for) the nation (if needed), 6) be loyal to the United States. (Ques.53)
We show loyalty to the flag when we say the Pledge of Allegiance. (Ques.52)

Two ways that Americans can participate in their democracy are: 1) join a political party, 2) help with a campaign, 3) join a civic group, 5) join a community group, 6) give an elected official your opinion on an issue, 7) call Senators and Representatives, 8) publicly support or oppose an issue or policy, 9) run for office, 10) write to a paper. (Ques.55)

The last day to send in a federal tax return is April 15. (Ques.56)

All men must register for the selective service at age eighteen (18). (Ques.48)

In the United States we believe in freedom to conduct business.

The economic system in the United States is: a capitalist economy, a market economy. (Ques.11)

_____

The following four questions relate to your specific state. If you are not sure of the answers, you may find the information on the following web sites, or page 124 (for the capital city of your state).
U.S. Senators:
www.senate.gov/general/contact_information/senators_cfm.cfm
U.S. Representatives:
www.house.gov/representatives/
Governors of the 50 states:
www.usa.gov/Contact/Governors.shtml
Capital of your state:
(See page 124 for a list of all state capitals.)

_____

(Ques.20) **Who is one of you state's U.S. Senators now?**
Answers will vary. (District of Columbia residents and residents of U.S. territories should answer that D.C. (or territory where applicant lives) has no U.S, Senators.

(Ques.23) **Name your U.S. Representative.**
Answers will vary. (Residents of territories with nonvoting Delegates or Resident Commissioners may provide the name of the Delegate or Commissioner. Also acceptable is any statement that the territory has no (voting) Representatives in Congress.)

(Ques.43) **Who is the Governor of your state now?**
Answers will vary. (District of Columbia residents should answer that D.C. does not have a Governor.)

(Ques.44) **What is the capital of your state?**
Answers will vary. (District of Columbia residents should answer that D.C. is not a state and does not have a capital. Residents of U.S. territories should name the Capital of the territory.)

Questions 88 – 100 relate to geography, American symbols, and Holidays.

88. Name one of the two longest rivers in the United States.
Missouri (River), Mississippi (River)

89. What ocean is on the West Coast of the United States?
Pacific (Ocean)

90. What ocean is on the East Coast of the United States?
Atlantic (Ocean)

91. Name one U.S. territory.
Puerto Rico, U.S. Virgin Islands, American Samoa, Northern Mariana, Islands, Guam

92. Name one state that borders Canada.
Maine, New Hampshire, Vermont, New York, Pennsylvania, Ohio,
Michigan, Minnesota, North Dakota, Montana, Idaho, Washington, Alaska

93. Name one state that borders Mexico.
California, Arizona, New Mexico, Texas

94. What is the capital of the United States?
Washington, D.C.

95. Where is the Statue of Liberty?
New York (Harbor), Liberty Island, New Jersey, near New York City,
and on the Hudson (River).

96. Why does the flag have 13 stripes?
because there were 13 original colonies, because the stripes represent
the original colonies

97. Why does the flag have 50 stars?
because there is one star for each state, because each star represents a
state, because there are 50 states

98. What is the name of the national anthem?
The Star-Spangled Banner

99. When do we celebrate Independence Day?
July 4

100. Name two national U.S. holidays.
New Year's Day, Martin Luther King, Jr. Day, Presidents' Day, Memorial Day,
Independence Day, Labor Day, Columbus Day, Veterans Day, Thanksgiving,
Christmas

WRITING VOCABULARY
(Words you must know how to <u>write</u>)

PEOPLE	CIVICS	PLACES	MONTHS
Adams Lincoln Washington	American Indians capital citizens Civil War Congress Father of Our Country flag free freedom of speech President Right Senators State/states White House	Alaska California Canada Delaware Mexico New York City United States Washington Washington, D.C.	February May June July September October November

VERBS	HOLIDAYS	OTHER (FUNCTION)	OTHER (CONTENT)
can come elect have/has is/was/be lives/lived meets pay vote want	Presidents' Day Memorial Day Flag Day Independence Day Labor Day Columbus Day Thanksgiving	and during for here in of on the to we	blue dollar bill fifty/50 first largest most north one one hundred/100 people red second south taxes white

READING VOCABULARY
(Words you must know how to <u>read</u>)

PEOPLE	CIVICS	PLACES	HOLIDAYS
Abraham Lincoln George Washington	American flag Bill of Rights capital citizen city Congress country Father of Our Country government President right senators state/states White House	America U.S. United States	Presidents' Day Memorial Day Flag Day Independence Day Labor Day Columbus Day Thanksgiving

QUESTION WORDS	VERBS	OTHER (FUNCTION)	OTHER (CONTENT)
How What When Where Who Why	can come do/does elects have/has is/are/was/be lives/lived meet name pay vote want	a for here in of on the to we	colors dollar bill first largest many most north one people second south

Practice Questions

1. Civics (History, Government and Geography) Questions

Each page has 6 study cards. Each of the first 2 cards (top of page) have one of the 100 civics questions you may be asked.

Read the question out loud and then try to answer it out loud. This way you will get used to the sound of the question and the sound of the answer. This will help you remember the question and answer. If you don't know the answer, turn the page and look at the answer. Study the questions every day. By doing this you will find that even the difficult questions become easy after a while. Have a friend or relative who speaks English study with you. Let your friend or relative read the question, and then try to answer it. Ask your friend or relative if you are pronouncing the answer correctly. Say the answer over and over until you are comfortable with it and have it completely memorized.

2. English writing section

The middle 2 study card on each page help you practice writing English. Read the words, or better yet have a friend or relative read them. On a separate piece of paper, write the words, either in printed letters or in long hand (script). Before turning the page, try to make a sentence using all of the words. Write the sentence. Check to see if you spelled each word correctly. Does your sentence match the sentence on the next page (more than one sentence is possible). Have a friend or relative read the sentence out loud and then practice writing it. As in everything else, the more you practice, the better you will do.

3. English reading section

On the bottom 2 cards on each page (closest to the bottom of the page) there are several words.

Read the words. When you think you can read each word, turn the page and read the sentence in the study card near the bottom of the page. If possible, study with a friend or relative. Have them comment on the way you are pronouncing the words. Listen carefully when your friend or relative says the words.

100 CIVICS QUESTIONS

What is the supreme law of the land?	**1**
What are two rights of everyone living in the United States?	**51**

WRITE THESE WORDS

taxes pay we	**1**
most people has the California	**51**

READ THESE WORDS

here pay	**1**
Abraham Lincoln a was President	**51**

100 CIVICS ANSWERS

the Constitution	**1**
freedom of expression freedom of speech freedom of assembly freedom to petition the government freedom of worship the right to bear arms	**51**

WRITE THIS SENTENCE

We pay taxes.	**1**
California has the most people.	**51**

READ THIS SENTENCE

Pay here.	**1**
Was Abraham Lincoln a President?	**51**

100 CIVICS QUESTIONS

What does the Constitution do?	**2**
What do we show loyalty to when we say the Pledge of Allegiance?	**52**

WRITE THESE WORDS

is here flag the	**2**
Presidents' Day February in is	**52**

READ THESE WORDS

want pay to we	**2**
senators where meet we do the	**52**

100 CIVICS ANSWERS

sets up the government, defines the government, protects basic rights of Americans	**2**
the United States, the flag	**52**

WRITE THIS SENTENCE

The flag is here.	**2**
President's day is in February.	**52**

READ THIS SENTENCE

We want to pay.	**2**
Where do we meet the senators?	**52**

100 CIVICS QUESTIONS

The idea of self-government is in the first three words of the Constitution. What are these words?	**3**
What is one promise you make when you become a United States citizen?	**53**

WRITE THESE WORDS

can vote citizens	**3**
on the dollar bill is Washington	**53**

READ THESE WORDS

to want we vote	**3**
Bill of Rights is the what	**53**

100 CIVICS ANSWERS

We the People	3
give up loyalty to other countries, defend the Constitution and laws of the United States, obey the laws of the United States, serve in the U.S. military (if needed) serve (do important work for) the nation (if needed) be loyal to the United States	53

WRITE THIS SENTENCE

Citizens can vote.	3
Washington is on the dollar bill.	53

READ THIS SENTENCE

We want to vote.	3
What is the Bill of Rights?	53

100 CIVICS QUESTIONS

What is an amendment?	4
How old do citizens have to be to vote for President? (***)	54

WRITE THESE WORDS

be can free people	4
vote can United States citizens	54

READ THESE WORDS

Flag Day what is	4
one right name of a citizen	54

100 CIVICS ANSWERS

a change (to the Constitution), an addition (to the Constitution)	4
eighteen (18) and older	54

WRITE THIS SENTENCE

People can be free.	4
United States citizens can vote.	54

READ THIS SENTENCE

What is Flag Day?	4
Name one right of a citizen.	54

100 CIVICS QUESTIONS

What do we call the first ten amendments to the Constitution?	5
What are two ways that Americans can participate in their democracy?	55

WRITE THESE WORDS

is state a Alaska	5
White House Lincoln the in lived	55

READ THESE WORDS

the be why first	5
White House in the who lives	55

100 CIVICS ANSWERS

the Bill of Rights	**5**
vote, join a political party, help with a campaign, join a civic group, join a community group, give an elected official your opinion on an issue, call Senators and Representatives, publicly support or oppose an issue or policy, run for office, write to a newspaper	**55**

WRITE THIS SENTENCE

Alaska is a state.	**5**
Lincoln lived in the White House.	**55**

READ THIS SENTENCE

Why be the first?	**5**
Who lives in the White House?	**55**

100 CIVICS QUESTIONS

What is one right or freedom from the First Amendment? (***)	6
When is the last day you can send in federal income tax forms? (***)	56

WRITE THESE WORDS

the pay for flag	6
red white blue flag is the and	56

READ THESE WORDS

Labor Day when is	6
come people many in colors	56

100 CIVICS ANSWERS

Speech, religion, assembly, press, petition the government	**6**
April 15	**56**

WRITE THIS SENTENCE

Pay for the flag.	**6**
The flag is red, white and blue.	**56**

READ THIS SENTENCE

When is Labor Day?	**6**
People come in many colors.	**56**

100 CIVICS QUESTIONS

How many amendments does the Constitution have?	**7**
When must all men register for the Selective Service?	**57**

WRITE THESE WORDS

to vote want we	**7**
American Indians Alaska lived in	**57**

READ THESE WORDS

first to vote be	**7**
largest state is what	**57**

100 CIVICS ANSWERS

twenty-seven (27)	**7**
at age eighteen (18), between eighteen (18) and twenty-six (26)	**57**

WRITE THIS SENTENCE

We want to vote.	**7**
American Indians lived in Alaska.	**57**

READ THIS SENTENCE

Be first to vote.	**7**
What is the largest state?	**57**

100 CIVICS QUESTIONS

What did the Declaration of Independence do?	8
What is one reason colonists came to America?	58

WRITE THESE WORDS

pay taxes citizens	8
one right Freedom of Speech is	58

READ THESE WORDS

the is south where	8
people to want why do vote	58

100 CIVICS ANSWERS

announced our independence (from Great Britain), declared our independence (from Great Britain), said that the United States is free (from Great Britain)	8
freedom, political liberty, religious freedom, economic opportunity, practice their religion, escape persecution	58

WRITE THIS SENTENCE

Citizens pay taxes.	8
Freedom of speech is one right.	58

READ THIS SENTENCE

Where is the south?	8
Why do people want to vote?	58

100 CIVICS QUESTIONS

What are two rights in the Declaration of Independence?	9
Who lived in America before the Europeans arrived?	59

WRITE THESE WORDS

in we Canada lived	9
Washington California south is of	59

READ THESE WORDS

we do where pay	9
north states most are in the	59

100 CIVICS ANSWERS

Life, liberty, pursuit of happiness	9
American Indians, Native Americans	59

WRITE THIS SENTENCE

We lived in Canada.	9
California is south of Washington.	59

READ THIS SENTENCE

Where do we pay?	9
Most states are in the north.	59

100 CIVICS QUESTIONS

What is freedom of religion?	**10**
What group of people was taken to America and sold as slaves?	**60**

WRITE THESE WORDS

here the for pay flag	**10**
Washington, D.C. President in the lives	**60**

READ THESE WORDS

are Senators the here	**10**
largest country is the what	**60**

100 CIVICS ANSWERS

You can practice any religion, or not practice a religion.	10
Africans, people from Africa	60

WRITE THIS SENTENCE

Pay here for the flag.	10
The President lives in Washington, D.C.	60

READ THIS SENTENCE

The Senators are here.	10
What is the largest country?	60

100 CIVICS QUESTIONS

What is the economic system in the United States? (***)	**11**
Why did the colonists fight the British?	**61**

WRITE THESE WORDS

can people most vote	**11**
New York City the most people has	**61**

READ THESE WORDS

vote people do when	**11**
Senators capital in the meet	**61**

100 CIVICS ANSWERS

capitalist economy, market economy	11
because of high taxes (taxation without representation), because the British army stayed in their houses (boarding, quartering), because they didn't have self-government	61

WRITE THIS SENTENCE

Most people can vote.	11
New York City has the most people.	61

READ THIS SENTENCE

When do people vote?	11
Senators meet in the capital.	61

100 CIVICS QUESTIONS

What is the "rule of law"?	12
Who wrote the Declaration of Independence?	62

WRITE THESE WORDS

Flag Day in is June	12
Adams President the was second	62

READ THESE WORDS

is the where North	12
north people has most the the	62

100 CIVICS ANSWERS

Everyone must follow the law. Leaders must obey the law. Government must obey the law. No one is above the law.	**12**
(Thomas) Jefferson	**62**

WRITE THIS SENTENCE

Flag Day is in June.	**12**
Adams was the second President.	**62**

READ THIS SENTENCE

Where is the North?	**12**
The north has the most people.	**62**

100 CIVICS QUESTIONS

Name one branch or part of the government. (***)	**13**
When was the Declaration of Independence adopted?	**63**

WRITE THESE WORDS

the for flag largest pay	**13**
freedom of speech is of one Right	**63**

READ THESE WORDS

elects Congress who	**13**
colors American flag the has	**63**

100 CIVICS ANSWERS

Congress, legislative, President, executive, the courts, judicial	13
July 4, 1776	63

WRITE THIS SENTENCE

Pay for the largest flag.	13
One Right is freedom of speech.	63

READ THIS SENTENCE

Who elects Congress?	13
The American flag has colors.	63

100 CIVICS QUESTIONS

What stops one branch of government from becoming too powerful?	**14**
There were 13 original states. Name three.	**64**

WRITE THESE WORDS

flag largest free is the	**14**
Right freedom of speech one is	**64**

READ THESE WORDS

Memorial Day when is	**14**
the was who second President	**64**

100 CIVICS ANSWERS

checks and balances, separation of powers	**14**
New Hampshire, Massachusetts, Rhode Island, Connecticut, New York, New Jersey, Pennsylvania, Delaware, Maryland, Virginia, North Carolina, South Carolina, Georgia	**64**

WRITE THIS SENTENCE

The largest flag is free.	**14**
Freedom of speech is one Right.	**64**

READ THIS SENTENCE

When is Memorial Day?	**14**
Who was the second President?	**64**

100 CIVICS QUESTIONS

Who is in charge of the executive branch?	**15**
What happened at the Constitutional Convention?	**65**

WRITE THESE WORDS

for vote taxes Senators	**15**
President Washington the first was	**65**

READ THESE WORDS

one does vote when	**15**
the elect people the Congress	**65**

100 CIVICS ANSWERS

the President	**15**
The Constitution was written. The Founding Fathers wrote the Constitution.	**65**

WRITE THIS SENTENCE

Senators vote for taxes.	**15**
Washington was the first President.	**65**

READ THIS SENTENCE

When does one vote?	**15**
The people elect the Congress.	**65**

100 CIVICS QUESTIONS

Who makes federal laws?	**16**
When was the Constitution written?	**66**

WRITE THESE WORDS

is state Delaware one	**16**
first President the Washington was	**66**

READ THESE WORDS

Thanksgiving what is	**16**
was a President Abraham Lincoln	**66**

100 CIVICS ANSWERS

Congress, Senate and House (of Representatives), (U.S. or national) Legislature	**16**
1787	**66**

WRITE THIS SENTENCE

One state is Delaware.	**16**
The first President was Washington.	**66**

READ THIS SENTENCE

What is Thanksgiving?	**16**
Abraham Lincoln was a President.	**66**

100 CIVICS QUESTIONS

What are the two parts of the U.S. Congress? (***)	**17**
The Federalist Papers supported the passage of the U.S. Constitution. Name one of the writers.	**67**

WRITE THESE WORDS

to want free be people	**17**
lived the in people Washington	**67**

READ THESE WORDS

Congress the is what	**17**
lived here George Washington	**67**

100 CIVICS ANSWERS

Senate and House (of Representatives)	**17**
(James) Madison (Alexander) Hamilton, (John) Jay, Publius	**67**

WRITE THIS SENTENCE

People want to be free.	**17**
The people lived in Washington.	**67**

READ THIS SENTENCE

What is the Congress?	**17**
George Washington lived here.	**67**

100 CIVICS QUESTIONS

How many U.S. Senators are there?	**18**
What is one thing Benjamin Franklin is famous for?	**68**

WRITE THESE WORDS

President Adams was	**18**
during come people Thanksgiving	**68**

READ THESE WORDS

South the in we lived	**18**
states are the in many south	**68**

100 CIVICS ANSWERS

one hundred (100)	**18**
U.S. diplomat, oldest member of Constitutional Convention, first Postmaster General of the United States, writer of "Poor Richard's Almanac," started the first free libraries	**68**

WRITE THIS SENTENCE

Adams was President.	**18**
People come during Thanksgiving.	**68**

READ THIS SENTENCE

We lived in the south.	**18**
Many states are in the south.	**68**

100 CIVICS QUESTIONS

We elect a U.S. Senator for how many years?	**19**
Who is the "Father of Our Country"?	**69**

WRITE THESE WORDS

one is Washington State	**19**
come to we the White House can	**69**

READ THESE WORDS

Flag Day does come When	**19**
is the United States country a	**69**

100 CIVICS ANSWERS

six (6)	**19**
(George) Washington	**69**

WRITE THIS SENTENCE

Washington is one State.	**19**
We can come to the White House.	**69**

READ THIS SENTENCE

When does Flag Day come?	**19**
The United States is a country.	**69**

100 CIVICS QUESTIONS

Who is one of your state's U.S. Senators now? (***)	**20**
Who was the first President? (***)	**70**

WRITE THESE WORDS

Senators vote the here	**20**
United States Canada north is of the	**70**

READ THESE WORDS

can be a citizen who	**20**
Bill of Rights is the what	**70**

100 CIVICS ANSWERS

Answers depends upon which state you live in. (District of Columbia residents and residents of U.S. territories should answer that D.C. (or the territory where the applicant lives) has no U.S. Senators.)	**20**
(George) Washington	**70**

WRITE THIS SENTENCE

The Senators vote here.	**20**
Canada is north of the United States.	**70**

READ THIS SENTENCE

Who can be a citizen?	**20**
What is the Bill of Rights?	**70**

100 CIVICS QUESTIONS

The House of Representatives has how many voting members?	21
What territory did the United States buy from France in 1803?	71

WRITE THESE WORDS

elect the citizens Senators	21
United States Mexico is of south the	71

READ THESE WORDS

people do vote why	21
lived many in the people south	71

100 CIVICS ANSWERS

four hundred thirty-five (435)	**21**
the Louisiana Territory Louisiana	**71**

WRITE THIS SENTENCE

Citizens elect the Senators.	**21**
Mexico is south of the United States.	**71**

READ THIS SENTENCE

Why do people vote?	**21**
Many people lived in the south.	**71**

100 CIVICS QUESTIONS

We elect a U.S. Representative for how many years?	**22**
Name one war fought by the United States in the 1800s.	**72**

WRITE THESE WORDS

is the Alaska state largest	**22**
New York City Delaware of is south	**72**

READ THESE WORDS

is in north the America	**22**
senators the has government many	**72**

100 CIVICS ANSWERS

two (2)	**22**
War of 1812, Mexican-American War, Civil War, Spanish-American War	**72**

WRITE THIS SENTENCE

Alaska is the largest state.	**22**
Delaware is south of New York City.	**72**

READ THIS SENTENCE

America is in the north.	**22**
The government has many senators.	**72**

100 CIVICS QUESTIONS

Name your U.S. Representative.	**23**
Name the U.S. war between the North and the South.	**73**

WRITE THESE WORDS

north of is Mexico Alaska	**23**
United States New York City the in is	**73**

READ THESE WORDS

capital a is the city	**23**
U.S. country is of what south the	**73**

100 CIVICS ANSWERS

Answers depend on where you live. (Residents of territories with Non-voting delegates or resident commissioners may provide the name of that Delegate or Commissioner. Also acceptable is any statement that the territory has no (voting) Representatives in Congress.)	**23**
the Civil War, the War between the States	**73**

WRITE THIS SENTENCE

Alaska is north of Mexico.	**23**
New York City is in the United States.	**73**

READ THIS SENTENCE

The capital is a city.	**23**
What country is south of the U.S.?	**73**

100 CIVICS QUESTIONS

Who does a U.S. Senator represent?	**24**
Name one problem that led to the Civil War.	**74**

WRITE THESE WORDS

south of Canada Mexico is	**24**
Independence Day during come	**74**

READ THESE WORDS

Independence Day when is	**24**
Father of Our Country is the who	**74**

100 CIVICS ANSWERS

all people of the state	**24**
slavery economic reasons states' rights	**74**

WRITE THIS SENTENCE

Mexico is south of Canada.	**24**
Come during Independence Day.	**74**

READ THIS SENTENCE

When is Independence Day?	**24**
Who is the Father of Our Country?	**74**

100 CIVICS QUESTIONS

Why do some states have more Representatives than other states?	**25**
What was one important thing that Abraham Lincoln did? (***)	**75**

WRITE THESE WORDS

Memorial Day May in is	**25**
President dollar bill Washington is the on the	**75**

READ THESE WORDS

country a is America	**25**
Senators the in meet capital city	**75**

100 CIVICS ANSWERS

(because of) the state's population, (because) they have more people, (because) some states have more people	25
freed the slaves(Emancipation Proclamation), saved (or preserved) the Union, led the United States during the Civil War	75

WRITE THIS SENTENCE

Memorial Day is in May.	25
Washington is the President on the dollar bill.	75

READ THIS SENTENCE

America is a country.	25
Senators meet in the capital city.	75

100 CIVICS QUESTIONS

We elect a President for how many years?	**26**
What did the Emancipation Proclamation do?	**76**

WRITE THESE WORDS

Independence Day is July in	**26**
New York City largest is the one	**76**

READ THESE WORDS

Presidents' Day when is	**26**
north the largest is the in state	**76**

100 CIVICS ANSWERS

four (4)	**26**
freed the slaves, freed slaves in the Confederacy, freed slaves in the Confederate states, freed slaves in most Southern states	76

WRITE THIS SENTENCE

Independence Day is in July.	**26**
New York City is the largest one.	76

READ THIS SENTENCE

When is Presidents' Day?	**26**
New York City is the largest one.	76

100 CIVICS QUESTIONS

In what month do we vote for President? (***)	**27**
What did Susan B. Anthony do?	**77**

WRITE THESE WORDS

Labor Day in is September	**27**
New York City Delaware north of is	**77**

READ THESE WORDS

city largest is the where	**27**
Abraham Lincoln name second is the	**77**

100 CIVICS ANSWERS

November	**27**
fought for women's rights, fought for civil rights	**77**

WRITE THIS SENTENCE

Labor Day is in September.	**27**
New York City is north of Delaware.	**77**

READ THIS SENTENCE

Where is the largest city?	**27**
The second name is Abraham Lincoln.	**77**

100 CIVICS QUESTIONS

What is the name of the President of the United States now? (***)	28
Name one war fought by the United States in the 1900s. (***)	78

WRITE THESE WORDS

Columbus Day in is October	28
White House the in is Washington, D.C.	78

READ THESE WORDS

President was the here	28
government the for is people	78

100 CIVICS ANSWERS

Barack Obama, Obama	28
World War I, World War II, Korean War, Vietnam War, (Persian) Gulf War	78

WRITE THIS SENTENCE

Columbus Day is in October.	28
The White House is in Washington, D.C.	78

READ THIS SENTENCE

The President was here.	28
Government is for the people.	78

100 CIVICS QUESTIONS

What is the name of the Vice President of the United States now?	**29**
Who was President during World War I?	**79**

WRITE THESE WORDS

want　vote to　the　Senators	**29**
United States　the fifty (50)　states　has	**79**

READ THESE WORDS

people　the when　vote do	**29**
citizens　how　many do　rights　have	**79**

100 CIVICS ANSWERS

Joseph R. Biden, Jr., Joe Biden, Biden	**29**
(Woodrow) Wilson	**79**

WRITE THIS SENTENCE

The Senators want to vote.	**29**
The United States has fifty (50) states.	**79**

READ THIS SENTENCE

When do the people vote?	**29**
How many rights do citizens have?	**79**

100 CIVICS QUESTIONS

If the President can no longer serve, who becomes President?	30
Who was President during the Great Depression and World War II?	80

WRITE THESE WORDS

White House the white is	30
President the in lives White House the	80

READ THESE WORDS

we the can meet President	30
country is what north the of U.S.	80

100 CIVICS ANSWERS

the Vice President	**30**
(Franklin) Roosevelt	**80**

WRITE THIS SENTENCE

The White House is white.	**30**
The President lives in the White House.	**80**

READ THIS SENTENCE

We can meet the President.	**30**
What country is north of the U.S.?	**80**

100 CIVICS QUESTIONS

If both the President and the Vice President can no longer serve, who becomes President?	**31**
Who did the United States fight in World War II?	**81**

WRITE THESE WORDS

north of is Delaware Mexico	**31**
Washington the is Father of Our Country	**81**

READ THESE WORDS

Senators here are most	**31**
Senators many in how are Congress	**81**

100 CIVICS ANSWERS

the Speaker of the House	**31**
Japan, Germany, and Italy	**81**

WRITE THIS SENTENCE

Delaware is north of Mexico.	**31**
Washington is the Father of Our Country.	**81**

READ THIS SENTENCE

Most Senators are here.	**31**
How many Senators are in Congress?	**81**

100 CIVICS QUESTIONS

Who is the Commander in Chief of the military?	**32**
Before he was President, Eisenhower was a general. What war was he in?	**82**

WRITE THESE WORDS

November in vote citizens	**32**
freedom of speech come people here for	**82**

READ THESE WORDS

the meet Senators we can	**32**
President is what the name of the	**82**

100 CIVICS ANSWERS

the President	**32**
World War II	**82**

WRITE THIS SENTENCE

Citizens vote in November.	**32**
People come here for freedom of speech.	**82**

READ THIS SENTENCE

We can meet the Senators.	**32**
What is the name of the President?	**82**

100 CIVICS QUESTIONS

Who signs bills to become laws?	33
During the Cold War, what was the main concern of the United States?	83

WRITE THESE WORDS

the to come White House	33
Congress one hundred (100) has Senators	83

READ THESE WORDS

what we to right is want do	33
Abraham Lincoln the in lived north	83

100 CIVICS ANSWERS

the President	**33**
Communism	**83**

WRITE THIS SENTENCE

Come to the White House.	**33**
Congress has one hundred (100) Senators.	**83**

READ THIS SENTENCE

We want to do what is right.	**33**
Abraham Lincoln lived in the north.	**83**

100 CIVICS QUESTIONS

Who vetoes bills?	**34**
What movement tried to end racial discrimination?	**84**

WRITE THESE WORDS

Canada largest is the state	**34**
White House the the has flag largest	**84**

READ THESE WORDS

city here largest the is	**34**
country is what the capital of the	**84**

100 CIVICS ANSWERS

the President	34
civil rights (movement)	84

WRITE THIS SENTENCE

Is Canada the largest state?	34
The White House has the largest flag.	84

READ THIS SENTENCE

The largest city is here.	34
Where is the capital of the country?	84

100 CIVICS QUESTIONS

What does the President's Cabinet do?	35
What did Martin Luther King, Jr. do? (***)	85

WRITE THESE WORDS

American Indians vote can	35
freedom of speech Right of have we the	85

READ THESE WORDS

was who Abraham Lincoln	35
President the the is citizen first	85

100 CIVICS ANSWERS

advises the President	**35**
fought for civil rights, worked for equality for all Americans	**85**

WRITE THIS SENTENCE

American Indians can vote.	**35**
We have the Right of freedom of speech.	**85**

READ THIS SENTENCE

Who was Abraham Lincoln?	**35**
The President is the first citizen.	**85**

100 CIVICS QUESTIONS

What are two Cabinet-level positions?	**36**
What major event happened on September 11, 2001, in the United States?	**86**

WRITE THESE WORDS

the is to Right one right vote	**36**
Washington Father of Our Country the is	**86**

READ THESE WORDS

is here White House the	**36**
Columbus Day Thanksgiving, when are, and	**86**

100 CIVICS ANSWERS

Secretary of Agriculture, Secretary of Commerce, Secretary of Defense, Secretary of Education, Secretary of Energy, Secretary of Health and Human Services, Secretary of Homeland Security, Secretary of Housing & Urban Development, Secretary of Interior, Secretary of Labor, Secretary of State, Secretary of Transportation, Secretary of Treasury, Secretary of Veterans Affairs, Attorney General, Vice President	36
Terrorists attacked the United States.	86

WRITE THIS SENTENCE

One Right is the right to vote.	36
The Father of Our Country is Washington.	86

READ THIS SENTENCE

The White House is here.	36
When are Columbus Day and Thanksgiving?	86

100 CIVICS QUESTIONS

What does the judicial branch do?	**37**
Name one American Indian tribe in the United States.	**87**

WRITE THESE WORDS

Alaska the largest state is	**37**
Lincoln during was President the Civil War	**87**

READ THESE WORDS

Labor Day here on come	**37**
United States many have people rights	**87**

100 CIVICS ANSWERS

reviews laws, explains laws, resolves disputes (disagreements), decides if a law goes against the Constitution	**37**
Cherokee, Navajo, Sioux, Chippewa, Choctaw, Pueblo, Apache, Iroquois, Creek, Blackfeet, Seminole, Cheyenne, Arawak, Shawnee, Mohegan, Huron, Oneida, Lakota, Crow, Teton, Hopi, Inuit	**87**

WRITE THIS SENTENCE

The largest state is Alaska.	**37**
Lincoln was President during the Civil War.	**87**

READ THIS SENTENCE

Come here on Labor Day.	**37**
United States people have many rights.	**87**

100 CIVICS QUESTIONS

What is the highest court in the United States?	**38**
Name one of the two longest rivers in the United States.	**88**

WRITE THESE WORDS

Thanksgiving in is November	**38**
Alaska the is largest the of 50 (fifty) states	**88**

READ THESE WORDS

the where dollar bill is	**38**
President the in the lives White House	**88**

100 CIVICS ANSWERS

the Supreme Court	**38**
Missouri (River), Mississippi (River)	**88**

WRITE THIS SENTENCE

Thanksgiving is in November.	**38**
Alaska is the largest of the 50 (fifty) states.	**88**

READ THIS SENTENCE

Where is the dollar bill?	**38**
The President lives in the White House.	**88**

100 CIVICS QUESTIONS

How many justices are on the Supreme Court?	**39**
What ocean is on the West Coast of the United States?	**89**

WRITE THESE WORDS

the elect citizens President	**39**
people United States come to the to free be	**89**

READ THESE WORDS

U.S. Senators the elects who	**39**
George Washington dollar bill the is on	**89**

100 CIVICS ANSWERS

nine (9)	**39**
Pacific (Ocean)	**89**

WRITE THIS SENTENCE

Citizens elect the President.	**39**
People come to the United States to be free.	**89**

READ THIS SENTENCE

Who elects the U.S. senators?	**39**
George Washington is on the dollar bill.	**89**

100 CIVICS QUESTIONS

Who is the Chief Justice of the United States now?	**40**
What ocean is on the East Coast of the United States?	**90**

WRITE THESE WORDS

citizens the Congress we elect	**40**
people American Indians want vote to	**90**

READ THESE WORDS

vote how citizen a does	**40**
George Washington President the was first	**90**

100 CIVICS ANSWERS

John Roberts (John G. Roberts, Jr.)	**40**
Atlantic (Ocean)	**90**

WRITE THIS SENTENCE

We the citizens elect Congress.	**40**
People want American Indians to vote.	**90**

READ THIS SENTENCE

How does a citizen vote?	**40**
George Washington was the first President.	**90**

100 CIVICS QUESTIONS

Under our Constitution, some powers belong to the federal government. What is one power of the federal government?	**41**
Name one U.S. territory.	**91**

WRITE THESE WORDS

White House the here is	**41**
President at the White House the meets people	**91**

READ THESE WORDS

the is where White House	**41**
Presidents' Day Memorial Day first come and	**91**

100 CIVICS ANSWERS

to print money, to declare war, to create an army, to make treaties	**41**
Puerto Rico, U.S. Virgin Islands, American Samoa, Northern Mariana Islands, Guam	**91**

WRITE THIS SENTENCE

The White House is here.	**41**
The President meets people at the White House.	**91**

READ THIS SENTENCE

Where is the White House?	**41**
Presidents' Day and Memorial Day come first.	**91**

100 CIVICS QUESTIONS

Under our Constitution, some powers belong to the states. What is one power of the states?	**42**
Name one state that borders Canada.	**92**

WRITE THESE WORDS

vote American Indians Alaska in	**42**
Citizens President Senators elect the the and	**92**

READ THESE WORDS

is Independence Day when	**42**
second President the lived south in the	**92**

100 CIVICS ANSWERS

provide schooling and education, provide protection (police) provide safety (fire departments), give a driver's license approve zoning and land use	42
Maine, New Hampshire, Vermont, New York, Pennsylvania, Ohio, Michigan, Minnesota, North Dakota, Montana, Idaho, Washington, Alaska	92

WRITE THIS SENTENCE

American Indians in Alaska vote.	42
Citizens elect the President and the Senators.	92

READ THIS SENTENCE

When is Independence Day?	42
The second President lived in the south.	92

100 CIVICS QUESTIONS

Who is the Governor of your state now?	**43**
Name one state that borders Mexico.	**93**

WRITE THESE WORDS

Adams the was second President	**43**
President Senators and taxes the pay the	**93**

READ THESE WORDS

capital in is the the north	**43**
capital the the city United States is of a	**93**

100 CIVICS ANSWERS

Answers will vary. [District of Columbia residents should answer that D.C. does not have a Governor.]	43
California, Arizona, New Mexico, Texas	93

WRITE THIS SENTENCE

The second President was Adams.	43
The President and the Senators pay taxes.	93

READ THIS SENTENCE

The capital is in the north.	43
The capital of the United States is a city.	93

100 CIVICS QUESTIONS

What is the capital of your state? (***)	**44**
What is the capital of the United States? (***)	**94**

WRITE THESE WORDS

one right the right to vote is	**44**
Civil War during the President the Lincoln was	**94**

READ THESE WORDS

in south name state a the	**44**
colors how many does the American flag have	**94**

100 CIVICS ANSWERS

Answers will vary. [District of Columbia residents should answer that D.C. is not a state and does not have a capital. Residents of U.S. territories should name the capital of the territory.]	**44**
Washington, D.C.	**94**

WRITE THIS SENTENCE

The right to vote is one right.	**44**
During the Civil War the President was Lincoln.	**94**

READ THIS SENTENCE

Name a state in the south.	**44**
How many colors does the American flag have?	**94**

100 CIVICS QUESTIONS

What are the two major political parties in the United States? (***)	**45**
Where is the Statue of Liberty? (***)	**95**

WRITE THESE WORDS

speech freedom of citizens want	**45**
American Indians in the lived first United States	**95**

READ THESE WORDS

lived here Abraham Lincoln	**45**
citizens America for the vote in government of	**95**

100 CIVICS ANSWERS

Democratic and Republican	**45**
New York (Harbor), Liberty Island New Jersey, near New York City, on the Hudson (River)	**95**

WRITE THIS SENTENCE

Citizens want freedom of speech.	**45**
American Indians lived first in the United States.	**95**

READ THIS SENTENCE

Abraham Lincoln lived here.	**45**
Citizens vote for the government of America.	**95**

100 CIVICS QUESTIONS

What is the political party of the President now?	**46**
Why does the flag have 13 stripes?	**96**

WRITE THESE WORDS

the the meets people President	**46**
capital the of is the United States Washington, D.C.	**96**

READ THESE WORDS

many south the has people	**46**
George Washington is why the on dollar bill	**96**

100 CIVICS ANSWERS

Democratic (Party)	**46**
because there were 13 original colonies, because the stripes represent the original colonies	**96**

WRITE THIS SENTENCE

The President meets the people.	**46**
The capital of the United States is Washington, D.C.	**96**

READ THIS SENTENCE

The south has many people.	**46**
Why is George Washington on the dollar bill?	**96**

100 CIVICS QUESTIONS

What is the name of the Speaker of the House of Representatives now?	47
Why does the flag have 50 stars? (***)	97

WRITE THESE WORDS

White House the is in the capital	47
American Indians the lived in first United States	97

READ THESE WORDS

many in people lived states	47
Abraham Lincoln United States was a President	97

100 CIVICS ANSWERS

(John) Boehner	**47**
because there is one star for each state, because each star represents a state, because there are 50 states	**97**

WRITE THIS SENTENCE

The White House is in the capital.	**47**
American Indians lived in the United States first.	**97**

READ THIS SENTENCE

People lived in many states.	**47**
Abraham Lincoln was a United States President.	**97**

100 CIVICS QUESTIONS

There are four amendments to the Constitution about who can vote. Describe one of them.	**48**
What is the name of the national anthem?	**98**

WRITE THESE WORDS

citizens taxes pay United States	**48**
President one lived Washington, D.C. New York City and in	**98**

READ THESE WORDS

George Washington who was	**48**
What the is of Father of Our Country name the	**98**

100 CIVICS ANSWERS

Citizens eighteen (18) and older (can vote). You don't have to pay (a poll tax) to vote. Any citizen can vote. (Women and men can vote.) A male citizen of any race (can vote).	**48**
The Star-Spangled Banner	**98**

WRITE THIS SENTENCE

United States citizens pay taxes.	**48**
One President lived in Washington D.C. and New York City.	**98**

READ THIS SENTENCE

Who was George Washington?	**48**
What is the name of the Father of Our Country?	**98**

100 CIVICS QUESTIONS

What is one responsibility that is only for United States citizens? (***)	**49**
When do we celebrate Independence Day? (***)	**99**

WRITE THESE WORDS

Washington, D.C. is Washington in	**49**
come before and Presidents Day Memorial Day Thanksgiving	**99**

READ THESE WORDS

the citizen first who is	**49**
George Washington father of our country the is	**99**

100 CIVICS ANSWERS

serve on a jury, vote in a federal election	**49**
July 4	**99**

WRITE THIS SENTENCE

Is Washington, D.C. in Washington?	**49**
Presidents' Day and Memorial Day come before Thanksgiving.	**99**

READ THIS SENTENCE

Who is the first citizen?	**49**
The Father of Our Country is George Washington	**99**

100 CIVICS QUESTIONS

Name one right only for United States citizens.	**50**
Name two national U.S. holidays.	**100**

WRITE THESE WORDS

Washington, D.C. in Congress meets	**50**
(100) Senators the Washington, D.C. vote in	**100**

READ THESE WORDS

to vote here a citizen has	**50**
largest city where is the in the United States	**100**

100 CIVICS ANSWERS

vote in a federal election run for federal office	**50**
New Year's Day, Martin Luther King, Jr. Day, Presidents' Day, Memorial Day, Independence Day, Labor Day, Columbus Day, Veterans Day, Thanksgiving, Christmas	**100**

WRITE THIS SENTENCE

Congress meets in Washington, D.C.	**50**
The one hundred (100) Senators vote in Washington, D.C.	**100**

READ THIS SENTENCE

A citizen has to vote here.	**50**
Where is the largest city in the United States?	**100**

HELPFUL WEB ADDRESSES

For current information on the following, please visit these web sites :

The names of the 2 United States Senators from your State:

www.senate.gov/general/contact_information/senators_cfm.cfm

The name of your state's Governor:

www.usa.gov/Contact/Governors.shtml

The name of your Representative and the name of the Speaker of the House of Representatives:

www.house.gov/representatives/

To visit the Immigration and Naturalization Services' web page, which includes information on the New Naturalization (Citizenship) Test:

www.uscis.gov/portal/site/uscis

STATE CAPITALS

Alabama - Montgomery	**New Jersey** - Trenton
Alaska - Juneau	**New Mexico** - Santa Fe
Arizona - Phoenix	**New York** - Albany
Arkansas - Little Rock	**North Carolina** - Raleigh
California - Sacramento	**North Dakota** - Bismarck
Colorado - Denver	**Ohio** - Columbus
Connecticut - Hartford	**Oklahoma** - Oklahoma City
Delaware - Dover	**Oregon** - Salem
Florida - Tallahassee	**Pennsylvania** - Harrisburg
Georgia - Atlanta	**Rhode Island** - Providence
Hawaii - Honolulu	**South Carolina** - Columbia
Idaho - Boise	**South Dakota** - Pierre
Illinois - Springfield	**Tennessee** - Nashville
Indiana - Indianapolis	**Texas** - Austin
Iowa - Des Moines	**Utah** - Salt Lake City
Kansas - Topeka	**Vermont** - Montpelier
Kentucky - Frankfort	**Virginia** - Richmond
Louisiana - Baton Rouge	**Washington** - Olympia
Maine - Augusta	**West Virginia** - Charleston
Maryland - Annapolis	**Wisconsin** - Madison
Massachusetts - Boston	**Wyoming** - Cheyenne
Michigan - Lansing	**U.S. Territories:**
Minnesota - St. Paul	**American Samoa** - Pago Pago
Mississippi - Jackson	**Guam** - Hagatna
Missouri - Jefferson City	**Northern Mariana Islands** - Saipan
Montana - Helena	**Puerto Rico** - San Juan
Nebraska - Lincoln	**U.S. Virgin Islands** – Charlotte Amalie
Nevada - Carson City	
New Hampshire - Concord	

?	Question 1

What is the supreme law of the land?

?	Question 2

What does the Constitution do?

?	Question 3

The idea of self-government is in the first three words of the Constitution.
What are these words?

?	Question 4

What is an amendment?

?	Question 5

What do we call the first ten amendments to the Constitution?

?	Question 6

What is one right or freedom from the First Amendment? (***)

Answer 2

sets up the government, defines the government, protects basic rights of Americans

 Answer 1

the Constitution

 Answer 4

a change (to the Constitution), an addition (to the Constitution)

 Answer 3

We the People

 Answer 6

Speech, religion, assembly, press, petition the government

 Answer 5

the Bill of Rights

? | **Question 7**

How many amendments does the Constitution have?

? | **Question 8**

What did the Declaration of Independence do?

? | **Question 9**

What are two rights in the Declaration of Independence?

? | **Question 10**

What is freedom of religion?

? | **Question 11**

What is the economic system in the United States? (***)

? | **Question 12**

What is the "rule of law"?

Answer 8

*announced our independence
(from Great Britain)
declared our independence
(from Great Britain)
said that the United States is
free (from Great Britain)*

 Answer 7

twenty-seven (27)

 Answer 10

*You can practice any religion, or
not practice a religion.*

 Answer 9

Life, liberty, pursuit of happiness

 Answer 12

*Everyone must follow the law.
Leaders must obey the law.
Government must obey the law.*

 Answer 11

*capitalist economy,
market economy*

? | **Question 13**

Name one branch or part of the government. (***)

? | **Question 14**

What stops one branch of government from becoming too powerful?

? | **Question 15**

Who is in charge of the executive branch?

? | **Question 16**

Who makes federal laws?

? | **Question 17**

What are the two parts of the U.S. Congress? (***)

? | **Question 18**

How many U.S. Senators are there?

Answer 14

*checks and balances,
separation of powers*

 Answer 13

*Congress (legislative), President
(executive), the courts (judicial)*

 Answer 16

*Congress, Senate and House (of
Representatives), (U.S. or national)
Legislature*

 Answer 15

the President

 Answer 18

one hundred (100)

 Answer 17

*Senate and House (of
Representatives)*

? **Question 19**

We elect a U.S. Senator for how many years?

? **Question 20**

Who is one of your state's U.S. Senators now? (***)

? **Question 21**

The House of Representatives has how many voting members?

? **Question 22**

We elect a U.S. Representative for how many years?

? **Question 23**

Name your U.S. Representative.

? **Question 24**

Who does a U.S. Senator represent?

Answer 20

Answers depend upon which state you live in.
(District of Columbia residents and residents of U.S. territories should answer that D.C. (or the territory where the applicant lives) has no U.S. Senators.)

 Answer 19

six (6)

 Answer 22

two (2)

 Answer 21

four hundred thirty-five (435)

 Answer 24

all people of the state

 Answer 23

Answers depend on where you live. (Residents of territories with Non-voting delegates or resident commissioners may provide the name of that Delegate or Commissioner. Also acceptable is any statement that the territory has no (voting) Representatives in Congress.)

? | **Question 25**

Why do some states have more Representatives than other states?

? | **Question 26**

We elect a President for how many years?

? | **Question 27**

In what month do we vote for President? (***)

? | **Question 28**

What is the name of the President of the United States now? (***)

? | **Question 29**

What is the name of the Vice President of the United States now?

? | **Question 30**

If the President can no longer serve, who becomes President?

Answer 26

four (4)

 Answer 25

(because of) the state's population,
(because) they have more people
(because) some states have more people

 Answer 28

Barack Obama, Obama

 Answer 27

November

 Answer 30

the Vice President

 Answer 29

Joseph R. Biden, Jr.,
Joe Biden,
Biden

? | **Question 31**

If both the President and the Vice President can no longer serve, who becomes President?

? | **Question 32**

Who is the Commander in Chief of the military?

? | **Question 33**

Who signs bills to become laws?

? | **Question 34**

Who vetoes bills?

? | **Question 35**

What does the President's Cabinet do?

? | **Question 36**

What are two Cabinet-level positions?

Answer 32

the President

 Answer 31

the Speaker of the House

 Answer 34

the President

 Answer 33

the President

 Answer 36

Secretary of Agriculture, Secretary of Commerce, Secretary of Defense, Secretary of Education, Secretary of Energy, Secretary of Health and Human Services, Secretary of Homeland Security, Secretary of Housing and Urban Development, Secretary of the Interior, Secretary of Labor, Secretary of State, Secretary of Transportation, Secretary of the Treasury, Secretary of Veterans Affairs, Attorney General, Vice President

Answer 35

advises the President

? **Question 37**

What does the judicial branch do?

? **Question 38**

What is the highest court in the United States?

? **Question 39**

How many justices are on the Supreme Court?

? **Question 40**

Who is the Chief Justice of the United States now?

? **Question 41**

Under our Constitution, some powers belong to the federal government.
What is one power of the federal government?

? **Question 42**

Under our Constitution, some powers belong to the states.
What is one power of the states?

Answer 38

the Supreme Court

 Answer 37

reviews laws, explains laws, resolves disputes (disagreements), decides if a law goes against the Constitution

 Answer 40

John Roberts
(John G. Roberts, Jr.)

 Answer 39

nine (9)

 Answer 42

provide schooling and education, provide protection (police), provide safety (fire departments), give a driver's license, approve zoning and land use

 Answer 41

to print money, to declare war, to create an army, to make treaties

?	**Question 43**

Who is the Governor of your state now?

?	**Question 44**

What is the capital of your state? (***)

?	**Question 45**

What are the two major political parties in the United States? (***)

?	**Question 46**

What is the political party of the President now?

?	**Question 47**

What is the name of the Speaker of the House of Representatives now?

?	**Question 48**

There are four amendments to the Constitution about who can vote. Describe one of them.

Answer 44

Answers vary.
(District of Columbia residents should answer that D.C. is not a state and does not have a capital. Residents of U.S. territories should name the capital of the territory.)

Answer 43

Answers will vary.
(District of Columbia residents should answer that D.C. does not have a Governor.)

Answer 46

Democratic (Party)

Answer 45

Democratic and Republican

Answer 48

Citizens eighteen (18) and older (can vote). You don't have to pay (a poll tax) to vote. Any citizen can vote. (Women and men can vote.) A male citizen of any race (can vote).

Answer 47

(John) Boehner

? | **Question 49**

What is one responsibility that is only for United States citizens? (***)

? | **Question 50**

Name one right only for United States citizens.

? | **Question 51**

What are two rights of everyone living in the United States?

? | **Question 52**

What do we show loyalty to when we say the Pledge of Allegiance?

? | **Question 53**

What is one promise you make when you become a United States citizen?

? | **Question 54**

How old do citizens have to be to vote for President? (***)

Answer 50

vote in a federal election, run for federal office

 Answer 49

serve on a jury, vote in a federal election

 Answer 52

the United States, the flag

 Answer 51

freedom of expression, freedom of speech, freedom of assembly, freedom to petition the government, freedom of worship, the right to bear arms

 Answer 54

eighteen (18) and older

 Answer 53

give up loyalty to other countries, defend the Constitution and laws of the United States, obey the laws of the United States, serve in the U.S. military (if needed), serve (do important work for) the nation (if needed), be loyal to the United States

? **Question 55**

What are two ways that Americans can participate in their democracy?

? **Question 56**

When is the last day you can send in federal income tax forms? (***)

? **Question 57**

When must all men register for the Selective Service?

? **Question 58**

What is one reason colonists came to America?

? **Question 59**

Who lived in America before the Europeans arrived?

? **Question 60**

What group of people was taken to America and sold as slaves?

Answer 56

April 15

 Answer 55

Vote, join a political party, help with a campaign, join a civic group, join a community group, give an elected official your opinion on an issue, call Senators and Representatives, publicly support or oppose an issue or policy, run for office, write to a newspaper

 Answer 58

Freedom, political liberty, religious freedom, economic opportunity practice their religion, escape persecution

 Answer 57

at age eighteen (18), between eighteen (18) and twenty-six (26)

 Answer 60

Africans, people from Africa

 Answer 59

American Indians, Native Americans

? **Question 61**

Why did the colonists fight the British?

? **Question 62**

Who wrote the Declaration of Independence?

? **Question 63**

When was the Declaration of Independence adopted?

? **Question 64**

There were 13 original states. Name three.

? **Question 65**

What happened at the Constitutional Convention?

? **Question 66**

When was the Constitution written?

Answer 62

(Thomas) Jefferson

 Answer 61

*because of high taxes (taxation without representation),
because the British army stayed in their houses (boarding, quartering),
because they didn't have self-government*

 Answer 64

New Hampshire, Massachusetts, Rhode Island, Connecticut, New York, New Jersey, Pennsylvania, Delaware, Maryland, Virginia, North Carolina, South Carolina, Georgia

 Answer 63

July 4, 1776

 Answer 66

1787

 Answer 65

*The Constitution was written.
The Founding Fathers wrote the Constitution.*

? **Question 67**

The Federalist Papers supported the passage of the U.S. Constitution.
Name one of the writers.

? **Question 68**

What is one thing Benjamin Franklin is famous for?

? **Question 69**

Who is the "Father of Our Country"?

? **Question 70**

Who was the first President? (***)

? **Question 71**

What territory did the United States buy from France in 1803?

? **Question 72**

Name one war fought by the United States in the 1800s.

Answer 68

U.S. diplomat, oldest member of the Constitutional Convention, first Postmaster General of the United States, writer of "Poor Richard's Almanac", started the first free libraries

 Answer 67

(James) Madison, (Alexander) Hamilton, (John) Jay, Publius

 Answer 70

(George) Washington

 Answer 69

(George) Washington

 Answer 72

War of 1812, Mexican-American War, Civil War, Spanish-American War

 Answer 71

the Louisiana Territory, Louisiana

? | **Question 73**

Name the U.S. war between the North and the South.

? | **Question 74**

Name one problem that led to the Civil War.

? | **Question 75**

What was one important thing that Abraham Lincoln did? (***)

? | **Question 76**

What did the Emancipation Proclamation do?

? | **Question 77**

What did Susan B. Anthony do?

? | **Question 78**

Name one war fought by the United States in the 1900s. (***)

Answer 74

Slavery
economic reasons,
states' rights

 Answer 73

the Civil War,
the War between the States

 Answer 76

freed the slaves,
freed slaves in the Confederacy,
freed slaves in the Confederate
states,
freed slaves in most Southern
states

 Answer 75

freed the slaves (Emancipation
Proclamation),
saved (or preserved) the Union,
led the United States during the
Civil War

 Answer 78

World War I,
World War II,
Korean War,
Vietnam War,
(Persian) Gulf War

 Answer 77

fought for women's rights,
fought for civil rights

? | **Question 79**

Who was President during
World War I?

? | **Question 80**

Who was President during the
Great Depression and World War
II?

? | **Question 81**

Who did the United States fight in
World War II?

? | **Question 82**

Before he was President,
Eisenhower was a general.
What war was he in?

? | **Question 83**

During the Cold War, what was the
main concern of the United
States?

? | **Question 84**

What movement tried to end racial
discrimination?

Answer 80

(Franklin) Roosevelt

Answer 79

(Woodrow) Wilson

Answer 82

World War II

Answer 81

Japan, Germany, and Italy

Answer 84

civil rights (movement)

Answer 83

Communism

? | **Question 85**

What did Martin Luther King, Jr. do? (***)

? | **Question 86**

What major event happened on Sept. 11, 2001, in the United States?

? | **Question 87**

Name one American Indian tribe in the United States.

? | **Question 88**

Name one of the two longest rivers in the United States.

? | **Question 89**

What ocean is on the West Coast of the United States?

? | **Question 90**

What ocean is on the East Coast of the United States?

Answer 86

Terrorists attacked the United States.

 Answer 85

fought for civil rights, worked for equality for all Americans

 Answer 88

Missouri (River), Mississippi (River)

 Answer 87

Cherokee, Navajo, Sioux, Chippewa, Choctaw, Pueblo, Apache, Iroquois, Creek, Blackfeet, Seminole, Cheyenne, Arawak, Shawnee, Mohegan, Huron, Oneida, Lakota, Crow, Teton, Hopi, Inuit

 Answer 90

Atlantic (Ocean)

 Answer 89

Pacific (Ocean)

?	Question 91

Name one U.S. territory.

?	Question 92

Name one state that borders
Canada.

?	Question 93

Name one state that borders
Mexico.

?	Question 94

What is the capital of the United
States? (***)

?	Question 95

Where is the Statue of Liberty?
(***)

?	Question 96

Why does the flag have 13 stripes?

Answer 92

Maine, New Hampshire, Vermont, New York, Pennsylvania, Ohio, Michigan, Minnesota, North Dakota, Montana, Idaho, Washington, Alaska

 Answer 91

Puerto Rico, U.S. Virgin Islands, American Samoa, Northern Mariana Islands, Guam

 Answer 94

Washington, D.C.

 Answer 93

California, Arizona, New Mexico, Texas

 Answer 96

because there were 13 original colonies, because the stripes represent the original colonies

 Answer 95

New York (Harbor), Liberty Island, New Jersey, near New York City, and on the Hudson (River).

? | **Question 97**

Why does the flag have 50 stars?
(***)

? | **Question 98**

What is the name of the national anthem?

? | **Question 99**

When do we celebrate
Independence Day? (***)

? | **Question 100**

Name two national U.S. holidays.

Answer 98

The Star-Spangled Banner

 Answer 97

because there is one star for each state,
because each star represents a state,
because there are 50 states

 Answer 100

New Year's Day, Martin Luther King, Jr. Day, Presidents' Day, Memorial Day, Independence Day, Labor Day, Columbus Day, Veterans Day, Thanksgiving, Christmas

 Answer 99

July 4

Other Books by Angelo Tropea

Non Fiction
Pass the New York Notary Public Exam
Pass the New York Notary Public Exam (Questions and Answers)
Notary Public Journal of Notarial Acts
Notary Public Journal 600 Entries
Notary Public Exam Speed-Study Guide

Pass the New Postal Test 473E 2010 Edition
Pass the New Postal Test 473E Second Edition

Pass the New Citizenship Test 2009 Edition
Pass the New Citizenship Test 2012 Edition
Pass the New Citizenship Test Third Edition
Pass the New Citizenship Test Questions and Answers (English, Spanish and Chinese Editions)
Pass the New Citizenship Test Quick Civics Lessons

Canadian Citizenship Test

Goldmine of Baby Names Boys and Girls
Goldmine of Baby Names Boys
Goldmine of Baby Names Girls

Aliens and UFOs: Case Closed
Zombie Pocket Guide

Cruise Fan Tips and Tricks

Fiction
Pinocchio and the Dragons of Martoon

NOTES